Building Capacity

Living in God's Abundance

JAMLIC MUNYASYA

BUILDING CAPACITY VOL.2
Copyright © 2024 by Jamlic Munyasya

All rights reserved.

No part of this book may be reproduced without written permission, except for brief quotations in books and critical reviews.

For more information contact
Jamlic Munyasya
Grace Dominion Chapel
Outering Road,
Next to Naivas Supermarket off Thika Road
Tel: 0712034747
Email: jamlicmunyasya@gmail.com

Printed in Kenya by
Tinta Image Communications
fpcomm@gmail.com

DEDICATION

The most wonderful and resilient woman I have ever met, my precious darling wife, Gladys. The

omniscient God knew my journey in life needed a strong shoulder to lean on. You were the oasis

of comfort when I walked through a thorny wilderness path. God bless you for me.

To my biological father - Senator Mutiso. Your wise counsel built the adversity quotient and

capacity to face the wilderness giants as I climbed a steep hill. I'm eternally indebted to you.

To you, dear reader. Develop your capacity for more as you delve into this wisdom.

PREFACE

Whilst this statement may sound outlandish and way off the mark, in the Kingdom of God we don't receive what we have asked for; on the contrary we receive what we can accommodate. Jesus gave a parable of servants who received talents in portions of five, two and one, respectively. The Master gave them talents each according to their ability and capacity.

The Unlimited God

In the Kingdom of God, we receive according to the capacity we have enhanced. The releasing end of God is unlimited, the receiving end of man is limited. Our unlimited God is able and will never run out of supply; however, we receive according to the capacity we have created.

God loves us equally but the flow of blessings will be determined by the measure we can accommodate. The three servants received gifts each according to their capacity. God is not unfair in the distribution of blessings. Our capacities betray us. The secret to accumulating more is increasing your capacity. No capacity, no flow!

Laus Deo

In the year 2009, my desire for communion with God drove me to join a team of brethren who were so devoted to the ministry of prayer. We spent three days of the first week of each month on the prayer mountain. Prayer became habitual and I devoted myself to prayer where I enjoyed heavenly encounters with Elohim.

Pile on the Agony

After six months of consistent prayers, I analyzed the impact of the fasting and I had nothing to show out of the many things I had asked from God. I began the journey of researching to discover why heaven was silent on such a committed and prayerful intercessor. A certain brother rebuked me for making lackadaisical and meaningless prayers. Later, he exposed me to pray scripturally. This inspired my confidence and I knew beyond a shadow of a doubt that I was entering my Kairos, a season of divine manifestation.

Out of the diligent study of the word and meditation to mine revelation knowledge, I grew spiritually and my prayer tempo was surging day by day. Many prophecies were released concerning the exploits God would do in my life but the earthly realm remained dry. I felt oppressed, subjugated, and subordinated. I got depressed and my faith in the Lord started sinking. With no one to encourage me, I encouraged myself in the Lord and built hope in the face of the great odds.

When Prayer Meets Capacity

According to science, conception occurs when a man's sperm meets with a female's ovum. Praise the Lord! Conception is impossible without the male and female in place. Prayer alone is not enough. Wonders are birthed when your prayer encounters capacity.

Five years later, God started answering the items one by one. I was elated to hear that heaven was concerned about me and that God had not forgotten His son. There was an overflowing grace that birthed the breakthrough I am enjoying today. From catch-22 to cloud nine, I was all over the moon. Ministry was in leaps and bounds, financially I was rising from break-even to breakthrough, and my career was blossoming. What a glorious season! I discovered the sense of my purpose and started maximizing my untapped potential. Glory to God!

Thorns to Roses

Heaven was open. I was inspired to delve deeper into understanding the kingdom's principles. Greatness is birthed in the womb of personal revelation. I needed heaven to reveal why the blessings were delayed for five years. So, out of curiosity, I began fourteen days of prayer and fasting. On the tenth day, I fell into a heavy trance and God began to minister to me saying "Son, I heard your prayers since the first day you started praying but you had not built enough capacity to accommodate the blessings." The issue is not heaven to earth but rather, earth to heaven. God will never deny anything good to the righteous, nonetheless, the release of blessings will be determined by what we can accommodate – capacity.

The Missing Ingredient

God heard my prayers, however, there was an ingredient that was missing – the capacity to accommodate. Your destiny is at the mercy of the capacity you have enhanced. If we can find this missing ingredient (capacity), heaven will supply resources abundantly.

Build Capacity

God does not waste resources. He only gives what you can sustain. The bigger the capacity, the more the outpouring of blessings from above. A supervisor who struggles to manage ten employees will face a rough path if more employees are added under his management. If God did not spare His only begotten Son, nothing good will He withhold from the righteous. Some of the delays we are experiencing are a result of our limited capacity. Like the widow in 2nd Kings Chapter Four, God wants us to gather empty jars.

This book is dedicated to helping my dear readers to recapture the essence and the missing ingredient; seeing beyond our eyes and living for the unseen. Our God is unlimited, the issue is our capacity. Your capacity determines your destiny.

TABLE OF CONTENTS

INTRODUCTION 1

Chapter 1
ENLARGE YOUR TENT 9

Chapter 2
DETERRENT TO BLESSING 17

Chapter 3
GATHER EMPTY JARS 23

Chapter 4
CAPACITY FOR KINGDOM RELEVANCE 37

Chapter 5
A LONE VOICE IN THE WILDERNESS 61

Chapter 6
THE MEASURING LINE 73

Chapter 7
WEAVE THE FABRIC 89

INTRODUCTION

What is Capacity?

Capacity is the amount of something that someone can accommodate. God does not give what we have asked for but what we have enhanced capacity for. Many people have spent years in prayer and fasting but cannot show what they have been praying for because there is no room to accommodate what they have been asking for. If the church is not taught how to enhance capacity, believers will live in mediocrity and not in the plan of God which is to change their lives.

The Assignment

In my book, *Building capacity Vol 1,* I said that Heaven is ever ready to release, sometimes even before we ask. However, the divine supply will be determined by the degree of capacity we have built here on earth. The widow lamented to Elisha about the terrible season she was going through and how everything seemed dark. The first assignment that the man of God gave her was to gather empty jars.

The Gift

I believe without any cloud of doubt that like Elisha, after asking, the next thing should be increasing capacity for what we have desired. The man of God showed sympathy and empathy to the widow. The plea to clear her husband's debt moved his heart although capacity was lacking. The best gift is teaching humanity how to enhance capacity for divine increase.

Spiritual ADD

We are living in times where every prophetic word is responded to with an "I receive." Surprisingly, there is no evidence of those things which we claim to receive because there is no room to contain them. God's blessings are limitless and abundant, yet our capacity limits their manifestations in our lives. While many believers are waiting for God to bless them, God is waiting for them to enhance their capacity to accommodate the blessings. God is able to do exceedingly and abundantly more than we could think or ask but this will only be fulfilled when He sees capacity. Some men are seeking God for greatness and elevation but when God looks at their capacity, He is limited to act.

Consider Solomon, who sought wisdom to govern Israel: God, impressed by his capacity, added to him knowledge and wealth. Delays in receiving blessings often stem from our failure to enlarge our capacity, causing God to withhold His abundant gifts.

Self-created Delay

Some of the delays we encounter in life are functions of limited capacities. My mobility was too much due to the mission engagements. I had so many challenges of moving to different counties for missions and as a student, I needed quality time with books as well. My pastor stirred up my faith which triggered my desire to acquire a car. That time I was a campus student, jobless with no stable source of income and I had no driving license. I lacked the capacity.

Even if God had blessed me with a car, how would I have driven it to missions? No driving license, not competent on the road, and no money to hire a driver. Though I needed it, my capacity limited me. Several years later, God answered my prayer. Sometimes God delays so as to prepare us for what He has prepared for us. It seemed like a delay but God intended to enable me to build capacity.

Seek ye!

I stopped praying about it and gave attention to the ministry and serving the Kingdom of God. To my amazement, God intervened and blessed the work of my hands and my dreams were actualized. I went to my devotional garden to thank God for the answered prayer. In my prayer, I asked the Lord, "Why did you take so long to respond to my prayer? You knew I needed a car for missions." The Lord answered me, "My son, I heard your prayer but you had not yet enhanced the capacity to accommodate the blessing of a car." Dear reader, God will never deny good things to the righteous. If He did not spare His son, He will withhold nothing good. We however receive according to the measure that we can accommodate. God was ready to answer my prayer but my limited capacity delayed the blessings. Some of the delays we are experiencing are caused by a lack of capacity. Destinies are delayed when capacity is not enhanced.

God will never deny good things to the righteous

Feather in the Cup

A parable of the Sower is told by Jesus in the book of **Matthew 13:1-9**. Of particular interest is **Matthew 13:8** which states, "But others fell on good ground and yielded a crop: some a hundredfold, some sixty, some thirty."

You cannot produce beyond your capacity. The capacity of an individual seed determines its yield. These seeds sprouted from the same ground but some produced one hundredfold, some sixty, and others thirty. The seeds reproduced according to their capacities. The seeds were provided with adequate conditions for production however, the yields differed because of their capacities. Water, fertilizer, and weeding were done and provided in equal measure for all the seeds but the quality and quantity of the produce differed because of differences in capacity.

In my book, *Building Capacity Vol. 1*, I said that God is not unfair in the distribution of His blessings. He has given us equal chances and opportunities but the results differ from one person to another because of capacity. If you take ten people and give them $10,000 as starting capital for a business, after three years they will be in totally different positions. The difference is caused by their capacities. Some people sit under a great man of God anointed to change people's lives but the change of the members differs from one to another because of their levels of capacity. Many people attended Jesus' sermons and teachings but their lives were not altered in the same way because of differences in capacities. The evidence of results that a believer is producing is determined by the capacity they have built.

Even Keel

We have even opportunities under the sun, yet our destinies and productivity are uneven. The productivity of these seeds was not determined by the farmer but by the capacity they had to bring forth the yields. Some people attended Jesus' healing and miracle services but went home the same. It is not because Jesus was unable to perform wonders but because their capacity limited the flow of oil. Some people move from one church to another because they are looking for blessings from God but the issue is not the church they attend but rather their capacity.

The grace of God has appeared to all men regardless of gender, race, tribe, complexion, wealth, height, size and age but the functionality of this grace is determined by one's capacity. God has no favorites; He gives us equal opportunities. However, the quality and quantity of results are at the mercy of our capacity. God has given every man twenty-four hours a day without favoritism. However, the produce and the results are in the capacity we have built. There are people whose time to break-forth came yet they are still in captivity because they have not built enough capacity. Some people live in mediocrity yet the purpose of God in their lives is greater but because they lack capacity, they cannot mount to such levels.

> *Destinies are delayed when capacity is not enhanced*

Moreover, you shall select from all the people able men, such as fear God, men of truth, hating covetousness; and place such over them to be rulers of thousands, rulers of hundreds, rulers of fifties, and rulers of tens. And let them judge the people at all times. Then it will be that every great matter they shall bring to you, but every small matter they themselves shall judge. So, it will be easier for you, for they will bear the burden with you.

(Exodus 18:21-22)

Moses was worn out by administratively judging Israel alone and he was required to delegate some of his duties to elders. However, the selection was not done through favoritism but on account of the ability(capacity) to judge. Of the many elders present among the Israelites, only those who had built capacity were given the mandate to judge. The success of these elders in their assignment to judge Israel was embedded in the capacity they had enhanced. There is no man that God chose for a particular assignment before measuring his capacity. If a nation is led by leaders who have no capacity for governance, the fate of that nation worsens. Even among the elders selected, their capacities differed from ruling thousands, hundreds, fifties to tens. Some ministers are seeking God for ten thousand members but they can only handle hundred members; therefore, they limit God to perform the desires of their hearts.

Chapter 1

ENLARGE YOUR TENT

God is willing to give us abundant blessings but our tents are too small to accommodate them. It is time for believers to quit prayers of "God bless me" to "God help me enlarge my capacity." God will respond to the amount of capacity we have enhanced. When you realize the place is too small to accommodate what you desire from God, then embark on enlarging it. In life, you will attract people of the same capacity. There are people you will never attract because of your capacity; men of capacity will attract men of capacity. Don't limit the blessings of God in your ministry, career, marriage, and business because there is no capacity to contain them. It is possible to carry an unlimited God and be limited on earth if you do not have enough capacity.

What's your Capacity?

There was a time I sought God to increase the members in our church but He asked me whether I could handle such a great number of members. I embarked on a journey of building capacity. A pastor who cannot manage a church of fifty members cannot handle five hundred members. No matter how much he desires and prays, there will be little or no manifestation on earth.

Roll up the Sleeves

Growth on this planet stops at the point where capacity stops increasing. People are fighting the spirit of stagnation in life but the issue is limited capacity. The moment we stop investing in growth is the moment we reside in stagnation. Nothing will change in our lives if our capacity is not changing. A proportional increase in capacity brings about proportional growth in a man's life. Destiny is a function of the capacity you have enhanced.

> *Destiny is a function of the capacity you have enhanced*

2 Peter 3:18 encourages us to grow in the grace and knowledge of our Lord and Savior Jesus Christ. Peter observed that the church was not growing in grace and the knowledge of the Lord. If the same revelation you used to preach in the early days of ministry is not changing, then it means you are not investing in building your capacity. As a believer, your knowledge about Christ should not be stagnant, it must keep growing daily. There are dimensions that God will never take us to until we invest in growing capacity. As a worship leader, you are required to update your playlist every time to ensure that you are growing. Some people start working in certain companies and firms but after several years fail to receive any promotion because they are not investing in enhancing their skills and knowledge.

God is Willing

The leper understood the efficacy of the eternal Son of God and the incredible greatness of His power. He said to the Son of God, "If you are willing you can heal and make me clean," *(Matt 8:1-2)*. In haste, Jesus said "I am willing." Even today, He is willing to elevate us. The grace for greatness is overflowing in the body but the capacity of an individual seed determines its yield. Even today, our eternal Father is willing to make us a wonder on earth. He wants us to walk in the platform of dominion but our capacity limits manifestation on earth.

If the same experience you used to apply in your workplace five years ago is not being upgraded, then you are not building yourself. Our investment in growth will determine our capacity. Growth is not an overnight event; you must spend quality time improving yourself. If capacity is being increased, there must be a change in your modus operandi. Some people have remained stagnant in all spheres of their lives not because there is a spirit opposing them but because they have not invested in enhancing their capacities. God is willing to release whatever we desire from Him but until we have created enough room it will never actualize.

> *Your destiny is at the mercy of your capacity*

Create Room

Enlarge your territories. Create room for what you desire. Abraham and Lot found themselves in a crisis of strife because of lack of capacity to support them and their possessions. The solution to this crisis was concealed in separation to create enough room. It was on account of this separation that God appeared to Abraham and promised him great blessings. The blessings of Abraham were not made manifest until he had created enough space. We are praying to God to give us great blessings and wealth but have no room to store the blessings. God will never release more blessings until He sees empty containers. There was no growth in the house of Lot and Abraham until they created enough space to contain more possessions. Weak capacity weakens your future. The greatness of Abraham was determined by the capacity he had built.

The Tragedy

It's a tragedy for a season to appear before one has built capacity for it. Some people encountered greatness before their time and ended up miserable because they were not prepared. Before Jesus began ministry, the Spirit led Him to the wilderness for training. If Jesus had stepped into this season before enhancing capacity, He would have not accomplished His assignment. Oftentimes young ministers are exposed to ministry before they are well equipped and end up being storytellers. Some men received elevation before they had enhanced capacity and instead of rising, they created a cloud in the horizon.

> *Any blessing we receive beyond our capacity is destined to bring calamity*

Face the Music

Anything that lands before your capacity has been enhanced will break instead of building you. Please hear me, my dear reader; never desire anything you have not enhanced capacity for. It will bring more harm than good. The prodigal son demanded inheritance from his father before he had built the capacity to manage it. Instead of making him, it destroyed him. Probably there is something you are pushing tirelessly and the manifestation is yet to appear, submit to the will of God.

Saul ascended to the palace before spending enough time in building capacity and this cost him the kingdom. God rejected his leadership and ended up dying desperately *(1ˢᵗ Sam 28: 17)*.

Private dealing for public proclamation

In my book ***Prayer that Works***, I said that before any public proclamation, there must be a private dealing with God. God found a replacement for king Saul, David, who had stayed in the wilderness enhancing his capacity. The problem with Saul was receiving greatness before building enough capacity to accommodate the kingship. David took fifteen years from the time he was anointed to be king before becoming the king. David spent all these years in the wilderness and cave of Adullam building himself before ascending to the palace. Before God announces you in public, He must have a secret dealing with you. In this secret dealing with God the capacity to contain greatness is generated. The greatest error King Saul made was rising to the palace immediately after receiving the anointing and never spending time in the secret place enhancing the capacity.

The Golden Wait

After an encounter with God, do not jump to open a church ministry. Take time in the secret place and enhance your potential. Jesus, being God never stepped out into ministry despite understanding He was powerful until the time God revealed Him to the world. Jesus took three years to build the capacity of His disciples to continue with the work of the ministry. He knew if He released them before time, they would be disappointed. Saul's failure to enhance capacity made him to engage in activities like consulting mediums which was not in line with what God wanted and this was the end of his kingship.

> *Before God announces you in public, He must have a secret dealing with you*

Stand the Test of Time

It's dangerous for a season to appear before you are prepared for it. Reuben missed the firstborn blessing because the man could not handle sexual lust and went ahead to sleep with his father's concubine. The blessings of God are given according to the measure of our capacity.

Chapter 2

DETERRENT TO BLESSING

Lack of capacity limits us. God's blessings are bountiful; however, He gives them according to our capacity to accommodate them. God will not give us blessings that will go to waste. The limiting factor therefore to our receptivity is not witchcraft or demonic altars but our capacity.

Don't limit God

The flow of divine deposits on earth is constrained by our capacities. When God discovers that no capacity in our lives can contain His blessings, He is forced to limit their release. Therefore, it is a call to the church to equip believers with the knowledge of building capacity to attract the blessings of God in abundance. God can never run out of blessings but He cannot release them when capacity is not enhanced. Some people blame the devil when they are not receiving the blessings of God but the issue is their capacity. The difference between you and the people who are experiencing God's abundance is the capacity. God has no preferences when He is distributing blessings; He only gives according to the ability we have. The problem is not the giving end but the receiving end. God does not require blessings in heaven, they are made for His sons and daughters but He will never release them until their capacity is enhanced. The degree of your elasticity will determine the number of blessings you can accommodate.

Expand your Horizons

God is unlimited in His workings. His wonders are unfathomable. However, He operates within the circumference of our abilities. In the early days of my ministry, I was so vibrant and the zeal to see the congregation grow was burning in me. Three days a week I prayed for church expansion. Countless times I visited my father in faith to sow a seed and seek impartation for growth.

One year later, I did a SWOT analysis of our ministry and indeed, there was no growth. In a year's time, only a handful of members were added. I had invested in fasting, door-to-door evangelism, and crusades. I even went to the extreme of making handbills yet all the efforts were futile. I cried to God with a lot of desperation hoping that He would change the situation but there was no change. I took some time in the quiet place and God asked me, "Son, if I give you fifty more members, where would you put them?" The eyes of my understanding were opened to see that God wanted me to expand the church by faith.

I immediately called the church executive to strategize on the church expansion plan. By God's grace, we built a structure that accommodated three times the congregation we had before. A month after this expansion, we began to see new members joining us every Sunday and then God began to minister to me, "My son, as long as there is capacity, I will keep on increasing you." Keep increasing the capacity.

God is Limitless

In *Building Capacity Vol. 1*, I asserted that in the Kingdom of God, we are ordained to receive more than we ask. **Ephesians 3:20** says, "Now to Him who is able to do exceedingly abundantly above all that we ask or think, according to the power that works in us."

God does not give us the exact measure of what we ask from Him but He desires to give us more. However, this is only made possible if there is enough room to contain the abundance. When we ask God for health, He has wealth and prosperity which He wants to add as a bonus but when He looks at our capacity, He is limited to perform. God can reveal Himself as Jireh, Shalom, Nissi, or Rapha at once but He is waiting for us to build the needed capacity.

Net-breaking Blessings

God is ready to give some of us great blessings but our nets are not enough to contain the blessings hence we end up limiting Him. God has instructed you to create enough space in your business because He wants to pour more blessings but there is not enough room for the blessings. The blessings that God has kept for us are very big but when He looks at our capacity, He is led to give us bit by bit. If you live in a one-bedroom house, the things you acquire can only be contained in that house but when you move to a bigger house you trigger heaven for more blessings.

No man can exhaust the provision of God

I understand that you have been fervently praying for the expansion of your business from a retailer to a wholesaler. However, it appears that the limited capacity you have allotted yourself may be hindering the full realization of such a blessing. Some ministers are seeking God for great anointing of healing and working miracles but their hearts are full of pride and bitterness thus limiting God to trust them with such anointing. This is because bitterness and pride are limiting factors for God to entrust men with greatness. There are people who, if God were to give them grace to heal the sick, pride would fill their hearts and this limits God from granting them access to higher levels of anointing.

There was a time when I fasted for many days seeking God for anointing to raise the dead and heaven was silent on the matter. God revealed to me that I had no such capacity at that time to contain the anointing. Some people, if given a chance to receive such a great anointing, will become dangerous to handle. Before you let down that net for the catch remember the blessings need nets. Enhance capacity!

Chapter 3

GATHER EMPTY JARS

The flow of oil continued until all the jars were filled. After reading the previous chapter, you see that there is a demand for larger capacities. How do I enhance my capacity for more? I'm glad you are asking.

i.   **Improve in character and integrity**

Man is an extension of God's hand on earth. The content of your character determines the height you hit here on earth. When Potiphar saw Joseph's character, he elevated him above everyone else in his house. Capacity for a higher position was sponsored by the content of his character.

This is demonstrated in **Genesis 39:5** which states that from the time that he had made him overseer of his house and all that he had, that the LORD blessed the Egyptian's house for Joseph's sake, and the blessing of the LORD was on all that he had in the house and in the field.

You can an the unlimited God but be limited on earth if you lack character. No matter how anointed you might be, if you lack character and integrity, you will be limited. Saul received kingly and prophetic anointing after Samuel anointed him and after he interacted with the group of prophets, respectively. He however could not sustain his kingly position. He could not sustain himself because he had not invested in his character. Your anointing will not be received by men if your character is questionable.

Divine Trust

God cannot trust you beyond your character and integrity. The trust of God towards a man is determined by the character and integrity he portrays. Some men have been seeking God for an overflow of blessings but their character and integrity limit God to bless them. Character refers to the moral qualities that distinguish one person from other people. Men are referenced on the account of their character because the real you is determined by your character. Many people guard who they are in public but their real selves are discovered in the secret. Your reputation is your shadow but the real you is your character. Integrity is the quality of a person being honest and having strong moral principles.

Many people will keep on praying and asking God for great blessings while God is waiting for them to build their capacity in character and integrity. God cannot use a man beyond the trust He has for them and this trust is earned through character and integrity.

> *God cannot trust you beyond your character and integrity*

To do righteousness and justice is more acceptable to the Lord than sacrifice.

(Proverbs 21:3)

Solomon revealed through wisdom that God is not interested in the sacrifices we offer for Him to trust us but rather, He cares about our character and integrity. There are people who have given great sacrifices trying to trigger heaven to release blessings but they have not acquired them because of poor character. Many believers cannot live without lies but they are busy seeking God for overflow. Character is the cup that holds the blessings; without it, you cannot hold them. God lost trust in Saul when he failed to walk in character and integrity. God rejected him not because He hated him but because there was no character and integrity in his leadership. God had to begin looking for a replacement- David, a man who had stayed in the wilderness and his character and integrity had been proven.

Some people are seeking God for promotion and elevation in ministry, job, and business but God seems silent because their character has not been proved worthy. Eli's sons had the chance to ascend to the priesthood after their father's demise but because they walked in wickedness, they failed the test and God had to raise Samuel. Opportunities will pass you because your character cannot be trusted. Before Jesus entrusted the disciples with the work of the kingdom, He stayed with them in seminars building their character. Gehazi had a chance of taking the prophetic mantle upon Elisha, but because of greed, the man lost this opportunity. No man has ever been trusted with greatness before God tested their character. Believers are struggling with pride, greed, and jealousy and this has limited their capacity to receive blessings from God. Some people cannot work without supervision because they cannot be trusted due to lack of character and integrity.

Paul, in *Philippians 4:8*, writes, 'Finally, brethren, whatever things are true, whatever things are noble, whatever things are just, whatever things are pure, whatever things are lovely, whatever things are of good report, if there is any virtue and if there is anything praiseworthy - meditate on these things.'

Paul admonished the church in Philippi to observe things that led to a godly character. Paul was trusted with great assignments because God had tested and approved his character. Some ministries have shut down because the leaders failed in integrity and character. Many people cannot be trusted with money because they have no integrity to handle money. Some people will never mount into leadership because the moment they get power they want to mistreat others.

Grace vs Character

You can carry an unlimited God but be limited on earth if your character is questionable. Daniel, Shadrach, Meshach, and Abednego purposed not to eat the king's delicacies. They were promoted to great positions of leadership in Babylon because they proved to be worthy. Before you become jealous in that company, business, or career because people are being promoted, ask yourself if you have proven your character and integrity. If we embraced a godly character and integrity as the church and nation, there would be no rampant corruption. Some ministers seek God for great anointing but when God looks at their character, He is forced to withhold the anointing. Anointing without character is destructive. An increase in content of character increases the capacity for more.

God will never invest His blessings in men who have not qualified from the school of character and integrity. Vashti's crown was taken from her the moment she failed the test of character. The king had to conduct an interview based on character to replace Vashti. The capacity to be trusted is founded on the character and integrity you possess.

> *Anointing without character is destructive*

ii. Increase in Knowledge

Knowledge is the awareness, skills, information, and facts that are acquired through education, investigation and observation. Our performance is determined by the depth of our knowledge and familiarity in a particular or specific field. You cannot perform beyond the scope of your knowledge. If a doctor is taken to a court of law to prosecute a criminal, he will flop because he has no knowledge of that specialized field. An increase in knowledge increases the capacity to perform. When a company is looking for employees, they are most likely to go for those people who have invested in a wide scope of knowledge.

If your curriculum vitae is not showing any attempt for growth, people will come and receive promotions while you sit there trusting God and praying for the promotion. No company will employ people who have no experience because productivity is determined by the experience and knowledge of the workers. We are living in a changing world in terms of technology and if you don't invest in growing your knowledge you will be frustrated when others are advancing.

Put out of countenance

I was invited to minister at a conference in Uganda. I was elated about the entire event since it was my first international ministry. I took two weeks of fasting and preparing to demonstrate the power of God at the conference. By the grace of God, I landed on the mission ground safely and set my feet on the pedal to transform lives.

Expectation is the covenant mother of manifestation. The church was expectant to receive international grace from Kenya. According to the program, I was to preach at least three sessions daily. Honestly, I was not used to this but I sought heaven for divine backup.

The first day was powerful. Glory to God! I noticed that as we came closer to finishing, I ran out of materials and I had nothing new to teach. I prayed for hours for God to supply me with the revelation knowledge of His word. The illumination knowledge to preach and teach is birthed by the head knowledge. I noticed I struggled because I had not exposed myself to the word of God. You can be prayerful but rhema comes from the revelation knowledge of the word. The last two days of the conference left me bewildered. I made a fool of myself.

After the mission, I decided to invest in the knowledge of the word. I started to have a diligent, consistent, and systematic study of the word plus serious meditation in a quiet place. Since then, I noticed that revelations flow like liquid. Glory to God! God's children perish due to the lack of knowledge.

Expectation is the covenant mother of manifestation

Mystery of the Arabian Desert

Paul's ministry was very effective because after receiving the encounter and call to ministry, he first went to enhance capacity through knowledge. He took three years to invest in knowledge. When Paul left Arabia, his ministry was the most effective compared to the rest of the apostles. After his encounter with Christ as he was heading to Damascus, Paul though an apostle disappeared to the Arabian desert to build more capacity which gave him a mileage in the ministry *(Gal 1:15-18)*. The twelve apostles, the disciples of Jesus, knew Jesus by interaction; Paul knew Him by revelation. His investment in knowledge gave him the capacity and comparative advantage over the other apostles to be the greatest author of the Bible. Paul effectively ministered to the Gentiles because he was very knowledgeable.

He wrote more letters than the rest because he was a man who was full of knowledge. The scope of your knowledge as a man of God will determine the effectiveness of your message to those who listen to you. Paul had knowledge of the tent-making business, law, and theology which gave him the capacity to write many epistles, more than those who had walked with Jesus. Paul had insight and revelation by the Spirit but he also invested in knowledge of the scriptures. The growth of our capacity is determined by the depth of our knowledge. The success of Paul's ministry was because the man invested in knowledge.

And Moses was learned in all the wisdom of the Egyptians and was mighty in words and deeds.

(Acts 7: 22)

Moses, while in the house of Pharaoh had invested in the knowledge and education of the Egyptians. This is why God chose him to stand before Pharaoh because he had the knowledge and wisdom of the Egyptians. Moses understood the language of the palace because he had been exposed to the Egyptian way of life, education and the proceedings of the palace. Being a stammerer, Moses avoided being God's spokesman. God insisted that he was His preferred candidate over Aaron because of his capacity. This man had acquired all the Egyptian education. God exposed him to the wilderness for training. If it was today in the Kenyan system, we would probably say Moses had a PhD in Egyptian law and culture.

> *The growth of our capacity is determined by the depth of our knowledge*

Capacity and Favor

Capacity and favor are covenant sisters. There are supernatural doors that open because of the level of our capacity. The apostle Paul did an authentic sermon in Antioch of Pisidia. The Jews and devout converts demanded a series of sermons *(Acts 13: 13-52)*. His capacity through knowledge of the word and grace of God opened a door for him to preach there again with Barnabas.

Some ministers are very anointed but there are platforms they can never stand on. Not because they are not favored but because they have not invested in knowledge. Knowledge is the secret that prosperous countries and governments have deployed – before you ascend to power, your level of knowledge is fundamental. The error of the third-world countries is that we elect leaders based on influence and wealth but not the knowledge they possess. The success of any organization, nation, company, or marriage is determined by the measure of the knowledge the individuals have.

Some people have become dwarfs in life with no sign of growth because they have neglected knowledge. Some men proclaim that anointing alone is enough to cause impact in the kingdom but the truth is that anointing must be blended with knowledge to make it effective. Many believers have remained stagnant in life not because God has not favored them but because they have failed to increase in knowledge.

You cannot operate beyond what you know

Stunted Growth

I listened to a certain general explaining how he lost his job. This man was working in an engineering firm. He trained and raised juniors who built the capacity to perfectly fit into his shoes. His juniors kept on growing in capacity and acquired more education. They acquired more knowledge. Eventually, the boss lost the locus standi because his juniors were more productive in the firm than him. No sooner had his eyes opened than the board of directors retrenched him. He mercilessly lost his job. What a tragedy!

Be a Reader!

Daniel was a reader. This is confirmed in **Daniel 9:2** where he says, "In the first year of his reign I, Daniel, understood by the books the number of the years specified by the word of the Lord through Jeremiah the prophet, that He would accomplish seventy years in the desolations of Jerusalem."

The captives in Babylon could have stayed longer than the specified duration if there was no man like Daniel who was a friend of books. The duration of their stay in Babylon was hidden in books and therefore it could only be known by men who were ready to invest in knowledge. Daniel understood that for him to get the secret of their stay in Babylon, he needed to explore knowledge through books. Daniel was a prayer warrior but his prayers were based on the knowledge he had obtained from books. The other captives were busy praying for God's deliverance but they did not know when the due time of their deliverance would be.

Hit the Books

If you are in business, employment, or ministry, you must increase in knowledge if you want to dominate. You cannot operate beyond what you know. Your level of knowledge determines the circumference of your operations. It's risky to operate without growing in knowledge. The destiny of these people was on the verge of delay until a man, Daniel, who was willing to get knowledge from the books of the prophets arose. Joshua's leadership in Canaan after the death of Moses was facilitated by ensuring the Book of the Law never departed from his mouth from which he meditated on day and night. God ordered him to study the Book of the Law to be successful. It is said that all leaders are readers. On your way to great levels of leadership, you must balloon the scope of your knowledge by investing in books.

The level of knowledge distinguished the ministry of apostle Peter and Paul. Although Peter had a direct touch and encounters with the Messiah, he would not write as many books as the apostle Paul who merely knew Jesus through revelation. Apostle Paul invested in knowledge more than the twelve disciples of Jesus, which was a plus.

Your level of knowledge determines the circumference of your operations
---

Chapter 4

CAPACITY FOR KINGDOM RELEVANCE

In my days of vanity, I have witnessed generals hit the ceiling and flop. Mighty men like Samson fall, relevant people lose relevance and their impact forgotten. In my book, *The Art of Consistency,* I said that Satan is scared of our consistency. Relevance is a function of consistency. Sustaining greatness is weightier than becoming great.

The Law of Time and Seasons

The greatest success of any man or woman is their ability to remain relevant throughout. Some people began well in life but flopped. Relevance is the ability to remain useful, important, or purposeful to the matter at hand or what is happening. Our significance in this world is at the mercy of the capacity we have enhanced. In a marathon, it is not how you start but how you finish the race that determines the winner. This is determined by the capacity you have enhanced in the training ground. If your absence in that firm, company, office, business, or institution is not noticeable it means you are losing relevance.

There are people whose one-day absence can affect the whole company because they have enhanced the capacity to remain relevant. We are living in a competitive world and if we don't invest in building capacity as believers, we will lose our significance, not only in the Kingdom of God but also in the marketplace. Jesus, throughout His ministry remained on the cutting edge because He had spent good years building capacity for the assignment. Jesus spent thirty years building capacity and did ministry for only three years and what He accomplished has remained relevant for centuries. Some people are forgotten within one month after their departure while others remain relevant for decades because they mastered the discipline of enhancing capacity in their days. One of the greatest inheritances we can leave to other generations is the ability to live purposefully and relevantly. Our greatest achievement on earth is the ability to remain significant for generations to come.

It is commonly said that if you see an old man making a mistake, don't laugh at them, learn from their mistakes. I organized a meeting with a general that God had used to birth revival in the village. I wanted to know how I could grow, influence and impact generations. I expected that he would lay his hands and impart the heavyweight grace that was upon his life during our meeting. When I sat down under his roof, the old man started shedding tears. He intently looked at me as he oozed wisdom and spoke sharp words that moved directly to the depth of my heart.

The old man said, "Son, the most important thing is the capacity to sustain and remain relevant all through." The sharp words pierced through my heart and my eyes flooded the floor with tears as the old man was speaking. He explained to me how he lost impact and relevance after birthing revival in the village. The capacity to remain relevant is more important than a one-day impact.

Be Equipped

> *"You are the salt of the earth; but if the salt loses its flavor, how shall it be seasoned? It is then good for nothing but to be thrown out and trampled underfoot by men. You are the light*

of the world. A city that is set on a hill cannot be hidden. Nor do they light a lamp and put it under a basket, but on a lampstand, and it gives light to all who are in the house. Let your light so shine before men, that they may see your good works and glorify your Father in heaven.

(Matthew 5:13-16)

After calling His disciples in **Matthew 4:18-22**, Jesus prepared a sermon on the mountain to equip them. He used metaphors to reveal what was required of them to remain significant on earth. Jesus never began by teaching them how to cast out demons, preach, prophesy, speak in tongues, heal, or perform signs and wonders but His sermon was about them remaining relevant all through. He knew all these things were easy for them but also knew that it was very important to sustain relevance.

Jesus, in His teachings, revealed that we are the salt of the world. The significance of salt is to add flavor to food and once it loses its taste it's thrown out and trampled by men. Jesus used salt as a metaphor to reveal the importance of you and me to the world. Many believers have lost their flavor and are no longer of significance in ministry, business, company, and offices. Salt is also used as a preservative meaning that if generations, companies, institutions, and governments will be preserved, there must be men who portray this characteristic of salt. Jesus also taught about another metaphor, light, which depicts our significance as children of God. Without light, no one can walk because where there is no light there is no direction. Light signifies direction and visibility and Jesus required His disciples to portray this characteristic as the light of the world. If we don't embrace ourselves as light, then the world will not know the significance of the church. If we do not reveal our importance as salt and light, then we will be failing in our mandate as outlined by Jesus. Jesus exhibited these characteristics and that's why His three-year work cannot be outlived.

> *Capacity to remain relevant is more important than a one-day impact*

Making Maximum Impact

> *At Joppa, there was a certain disciple named Tabitha, which is translated Dorcas. This woman was full of good works and charitable deeds which she did. But it happened in those days that she became sick and died. When they had washed her, they laid her in an upper*

room. And since Lydda was near Joppa, and the disciples had heard that Peter was there, they sent two men to him, imploring him not to delay in coming to them. Then Peter arose and went with them. When he had come, they brought him to the upper room. And all the widows stood by him weeping, showing the tunics and garments which Dorcas had made while she was with them. But Peter put them all out and knelt down and prayed. And turning to the body he said, "Tabitha, arise." And she opened her eyes, and when she saw Peter, she sat up.

(Acts 9:36-40)

Tabitha's significance in Joppa was evident and could not be denied. She was so important to the community that her death caused the whole town to mourn. The people had to look for Peter to come and bring her back to life because her position could not be filled by anyone. The absence of Tabitha (Dorcas) was greatly felt and could not be filled by anyone at that moment in Joppa. She understood her assignment well and had built enough capacity which made her remain significant to her community. God has called each one of us to add value to the world in businesses, companies, institutions, communities, and nations.

The relevance of Tabitha determined her coming back to life, not because Peter was powerful and anointed but because someone who added value to society had died. It's good to evaluate yourself on the kind of value you add to that marriage, company, institution, society, or ministry. If there is nothing, then embark on building capacity for relevance. If people cannot feel your impact, then there is a need to spend time enhancing your capacity. If people will have nothing to remember you with once you are long gone, then it means you wasted your relevance on earth. Peter was very significant to the church to the extent that his arrest provoked the whole church to gather in prayer for him because his importance was paramount. The reason why people who came after you in that company are receiving promotions before you is because the employer has seen their distinct capabilities – they have built the capacity.

Understanding Times and Seasons

The ability to remain relevant throughout is determined by how well you master times and seasons. God has not called us to remain relevant in a certain season and irrelevant in another. His delight is to see us relevant throughout generations. If however we do not understand times and seasons well, we may end up living in mediocrity. Sometimes God blesses people with riches and abundance but because they do not discern changes in times and seasons, they end up in mediocrity and poverty.

The scripture in *1 Chronicles 12:32* talks of the sons of Issachar who were always more advantaged than the rest of the Israelites because they understood times and seasons. These men were always prepared so that even during hard times they still prospered because they knew times and seasons change. No one will remain young forever, therefore, if you have this understanding you will invest in the days of your youth so that in the old days you will still be significant. If a man lacks the understanding of times and seasons like the sons of Issachar, then his generation is in danger. It is a tragedy for your generation to hear that their grandfather was the wealthiest man in society while they languish in poverty because you failed to understand times and seasons.

Jesus wept

There are three times that Jesus wept in the Bible. One of them was after observing the ignorance of men in Jerusalem.

> *Now as He drew near, He saw the city and wept over it, saying, "If you had known, even you, especially in this your day, the things that make for your peace! But now they are hidden from your eyes. For days will come upon you when your enemies will build an embankment around you, surround you and close you in on every side, and level you, and your children within you, to the ground; and they will not leave in you one stone upon another, because you did not know the time of your visitation."*
>
> *(Luke 19:41-44)*

Jesus was not an emotional man but when He entered Jerusalem, He wept over the city because they had no understanding of times and seasons. The eyes of the men and women of Jerusalem were blind when it came to understanding the times and seasons of visitation. It was this weakness that led Jesus to weep and prophesy terrible things that would happen to the city. Jesus warned them of the danger of falling into the hands of their enemies, not because God hated them but because their eyes were blind to understand times and seasons. Jesus revealed that this ignorance that the city portrayed would not only affect that generation but also their children. This reveals that some children are suffering because their parents failed to understand the times and seasons. What gave the enemies of Jerusalem an advantage was the inability of the men of Jerusalem to understand times. Jesus had occasionally taught His disciples about the end times and dangers thereof. However, He ensured that they were not ignorant of the importance of times and seasons for them to remain relevant when that time came. The world is evolving and developing at a very high rate, and if we will be relevant in the next few years, we must learn to understand times and seasons. Some people were very successful and relevant but after a few years, they were forgotten simply because they failed to learn the trends of various times and seasons.

Redeeming Time

> *Therefore, He says: "Awake, you who sleep, arise from the dead, and Christ will give you light." See then that you walk circumspectly, not as fools but as wise, redeeming the time, because the days are evil. Therefore, do not be unwise, but understand what the will of the Lord is.*
>
> *(Ephesians 5:15-17)*

Paul warned the Ephesian church about the evil world they lived in. He assured them that the advantage in those days was in redeeming time. The greatest tragedy is sleeping while the times expect you to be awake. Lacking this understanding will make you lose relevance. Wisdom is obtained when we understand how to walk circumspectly, knowing the days are evil. The greatest advantage and gift that you can ask from God is to understand times and seasons.

Seven gaunt cows, seven lean cows

Pharaoh had a terrifying yet amazing dream. It needed a man full of the Holy Spirit to give the accurate revelation.

> *Then Pharaoh said to Joseph: "Behold, in my dream I stood on the bank of the river. Suddenly seven cows came up out of the river, fine-looking and fat, and they fed in the meadow. Then behold, seven other cows came up after them, poor and very ugly and gaunt, such ugliness as I have never seen in all the land of Egypt. And the gaunt and ugly cows ate up the first seven, the fat cows. When they had eaten them up, no one would have known that they had eaten them, for they were just as ugly as at the beginning. So, I awoke. Also I saw in my dream, and suddenly seven heads came up on one stalk, full and good.* [23] *Then*

behold, seven heads, withered, thin, and blighted by the east wind, sprang up after them. And the thin heads devoured the seven good heads. So, I told this to the magicians, but there was no one who could explain it to me." Then Joseph said to Pharaoh, "The dreams of Pharaoh are one; God has shown Pharaoh what He is about to do: The seven good cows are seven years, and the seven good heads are seven years; the dreams are one. And the seven thin and ugly cows which came up after them are seven years, and the seven empty heads blighted by the east wind are seven years of famine. This is the thing which I have spoken to Pharaoh. God has shown Pharaoh what He is about to do. Indeed seven years of great plenty will come throughout all the land of Egypt; but after them seven years of famine will arise, and all the plenty will be forgotten in the land of Egypt, and the famine will deplete the land. So the plenty will not be known in the land because of the famine following, for it will be very severe.

(Genesis 41:17-31)

> *The investments you make in the season of abundance will determine your survival in the season of famine*

Pharaoh was in dire straits. Pharaoh's dreams looked complicated but when Joseph revealed them it was clear God was talking about times and seasons. If there had been no interpretation, then Egypt could have been in a great crisis. After giving the interpretation, Joseph suggested how to solve the crisis. He suggested measures of saving that were to be employed during the years of abundance so that in the season of famine there would be plenty.

The Revelation

Two seasons must appear in a man's life. In one season you experience abundance but the other season is famine. Therefore, the investments you make in the season of abundance will determine your survival in the season of famine. The problem with Pharaoh's dreams was not interpretation alone. The dreams needed a person who had a good understanding of times and seasons and what needed to be done to mitigate against the crisis. In life, the season of abundance will precede the season of famine. How well you handle the season of abundance will thus determine whether you remain relevant in the season of famine.

The Season of Abundance vs The season of famine

Every time you see the rainy season (abundance) always know there will be a dry season (famine). If you don't build the capacity during the season of abundance, you will become irrelevant when famine knocks at the door. There are people today who were once rich and everyone celebrated them in the society. However, they were not wise and are now irrelevant and in poverty because they failed to understand times and seasons. Samson woke up one day thinking he would slay the Philistines as usual but he never knew that strength had departed from him. Years can eat years so that the years of abundance are forgotten if we fail to understand times and seasons. When you realize everything around you is doing well, remember a season of famine is coming and how you survive in the days of adversity will be determined by the capacity you enhanced in the season of abundance. Some believers were giants in faith and business but they failed to build capacity in their days of abundance and ended up in tears.

Remember now your Creator in the days of your youth, before the difficult days come, and the years draw near when you say, "I have no pleasure in them": While the sun and the light, the moon and the stars, are not darkened, and the clouds do not return after the rain.

(Ecclesiastes 12:1-2)

Solomon, in his wisdom, admonished the youths to be committed to serving God while strength remained because days would come when they would be willing to serve but they would be unable to. Those who joke in the season of abundance end up irrelevant. The worst phrase in a man's life is "I wish I knew." Therefore, to avoid it in the season of famine, build capacity in the season of abundance.

Years can eat years

WAYS OF REMAINING RELEVANT

1. Establish a Covenant with God

A covenant is an agreement between two people. Two people cannot walk together unless they agree. For God to walk with a man there must be an agreement *(Amos 3:3)*. The secret of a covenant is what kept the giants of faith and their generations. When God blessed Abraham with wealth and many descendants, Abraham ensured there was a covenant between him and God for the sake of the days of adversity. Abraham knew that a season would come when his people would be in adversity and the only escape route was through establishing a covenant with God. Many people tend to drift away from God after His blessings without understanding that the days of adversity lie ahead of them. Oftentimes, people humble and pray when they want blessings from God. Once they acquire them, they forget God until the season of famine comes knocking at the door and they have nowhere to run.

The Israelites found themselves in the hands of the Egyptians and they began to suffer afflictions and hardships. For four hundred years the descendants of Abraham were held captive in a foreign land. *Exodus 2:24* tells us that when God remembered the covenant He had entered into with Abraham, He began a mission of deliverance; not because they were holy but because there was a covenant speaking. Covenants are paths of preservation for us and our generations. Pharaoh had devised means of afflicting and finishing off the Israelites but because there was a covenant that was speaking, they were preserved. A time will come when you cannot pray or fight your enemies and that is the time when the covenants you made with God will defend you. What will defend you at the moment when strength fails is the covenant you established with God in your season of abundance.

2. Build Quality Relationships

When God has remembered you and everything seems well, do not turn your back on other men because you will need them in the days of adversity. In the season of abundance, build quality relationships. Jesus was the son of God but He needed Simon of Cyrene to support Him in carrying the cross on His way to Golgotha. Some people had good friends but when God elevated them, they forsook those friends without an understanding that a season of adversity comes. Jonathan built a quality relationship with David who was a shepherd. A time came when Jonathan died and David was the king of Israel. Saul's household was diminishing and David remembered his friendship and covenant with Jonathan. For the sake of this friendship, he rescued Jonathan's son, Mephibosheth. Jonathan's generation would have been forgotten but his friendship with David preserved it. When God has remembered you don't delete other people's numbers or ignore their calls. A season will come when you need their help. Jonathan, even without predicting his demise from the face of the earth, entered into a quality relationship with David and through this, his family remained relevant. Men are doors that God uses to bless other men, be careful how you handle men.

> *Then they came to Him, bringing a paralytic who was carried by four men. And when they could not come near Him because of the crowd, they uncovered the roof where He was. So when they had broken through, they let down the bed on which the paralytic was lying. When Jesus saw their faith, He said to the paralytic, "Son, your sins are forgiven you."*
>
> *(Mark 2:3-5)*

The paralytic man had no strength to access Jesus but he had four friends who were ready to sacrifice their time and even open the roof and drop him where Jesus was. In life, you need such people who are ready to stand with you when no one else can. If this man had failed to have friends when he was healthy, he would have died in that sick bed. Some people claim that when they have God, they need no men but they forget God will use men to bless them. No man is an island.

3. Invest in Transforming Others

In the Kingdom of God, we grow through lifting others. In the season of abundance, when God has elevated you and everything is working in your favor, lift men. Selflessly invest in transforming other people's lives. It was in the season of abundance that a prince stooped low and invested in protecting and lifting a shepherd. Jonathan the prince, King Saul's son, never knew that at some point the shepherd he invested in would become a king. Never celebrate at the top alone. You need pillars to sustain you there. Become an open door for men to get job opportunities. It's so dangerous to be at the top alone. The relationships you establish in the season of abundance are the channels and pillars that will support you in the season of famine.

> *The relationships you establish in the season of abundance are the channels and pillars that will support you in the season of famine*

Never grow alone, ensure you rise with other people. The people you transform in your rising become your pillars in your time of need. Everyone needs pillars in life, people who can lend a hand in times of adversity. Selfish people aim at becoming superstars in ministry, companies, and institutions yet they end up desperate because they lack people who can come through for them since they failed to invest in lifting others. There are people raised to high positions by God but the people around them are living in desperation because they are self-centered. The greatest desire and prayer for the members that God has put under my shepherdhood is to see them grow to greater levels. If God has given you a chance to dine with kings and be in a position to help other people, don't be selfish. The capacity you build in that season by investing in others will make you sustain your relevance in times of adversity. When God has graced you, be a destiny helper to others because they will remember you in your days of famine. Jesus invested in raising men of His kind so that there was no gap noticed after His ascension. When Peter saw how they treated Jesus, he chopped off one of the soldier's ears because he knew the kind of investment Jesus had made in them. If you invest in men in their dark days, they will remember you in their days of glory. A candle does not lose anything by lighting other candles.

4. Invest in Heaven and on Earth

In the days of abundance do not eat everything, be sure to invest. People who fear to invest struggle in the seasons of famine. After God has given a great harvest do not eat the seed because you will need it in the sowing season. Any investment pertaining to prayer, wealth, income, talent and service in the Kingdom of God attracts wages.

> *But lay up for yourselves treasures in heaven, where neither moth nor rust destroys and where thieves do not break in and steal.*
>
> *(Matthew 6:20)*

Jesus advised His disciples of the importance of investing in heaven where there is maximum security from the devourers. Whenever God blesses us with wealth it is important to invest in the kingdom so that when adversity arises, God will secure us and protect everything we have accumulated. Joseph advised Pharaoh to have an investment plan during the seven years of abundance so that in the season of famine the investment would serve them. It is an error as a parent to walk in divine prosperity and allow your generation to suffer because you were ignorant about putting up investments on earth and in heaven. If the generations to come will not suffer in the season of famine, then the current generation must understand the concept of investing both on earth and in heaven. The greatest inheritance we can give to our generations to help them in the days of adversity is teaching them the culture of investing on earth and in heaven.

> *Go to the ant, you sluggard! Consider her ways and be wise, which, having no captain, overseer or ruler, provides her supplies in the summer, and gathers her food in the harvest.*
>
> *(Proverbs 6:6-8)*
>
> *Cast your bread upon the waters, for you will find it after many days. Give a serving to seven, and also to eight, for you do not know what evil will be on the earth. If the clouds are full of rain, they empty themselves upon the earth;*
>
> *(Ecclesiastes 11:1-3a)*

Solomon had observed the saving and investment culture of ants. The ants gather up food in the season of harvest and store it so that in the summer they have plenty of supply. It is hard to find ants starving in the season of famine because they understand the culture of saving during the season of abundance. Solomon gives us the wisdom of casting bread in many waters.

This means investing because we don't know what will happen tomorrow. The investment we make today will determine our relevance tomorrow. Investment can be likened to the evaporation of water into the skies: once full it empties itself as rain(blessings). Solomon teaches us that evil days are bound to come but to survive them there must be an investment that we have cast in many waters. No investment is a waste; it will always come back, especially in the days of famine. Many people after getting money want to spend it on pleasure without the knowledge that evil days will come. Before you spend everything that God has given you, develop an investment culture; it will save you in the days of famine. The most successful people I have met have one thing in common, an investment culture.

5. Do something to be a memorial before God

When you find yourself in a position to do something for the sake of the kingdom, don't run from this because when evil days befall you, it will be set as a reminder before God. Some people have been in church for decades but have done nothing that they can remind God of when they are faced with challenges.

Everything good we do in the kingdom; choir, ushering, cleaning and arranging the church, praise and worship, intercessory, and evangelism is recorded in heaven as a reminder to God in the days of adversity. You may not do great things that men can recognize but ensure they are recognized in heaven so that when evil days come, they will be a memorial before God.

Mordecai was facing accusations and death from Haman, the enemy of the Jews. Haman was powerful and had all the resources to obliterate Mordecai; however, Mordecai had a record of good things he did for the king when his enemies wanted to kill him. The book of *Esther 6:1* says that on that night the king could not sleep. One was commanded to bring the book of the records of the chronicles, and they were read before the king. When the book of remembrance was opened, Mordecai was delivered from the wrath of Haman and was honored. Mordecai had no defence before Haman, but something he had done served as a reminder to the king and he was rescued. There is a time you will find yourself in that sickbed where the doctors can do nothing; the only thing that will save you besides God's mercy, is what you can remind God of.

Chapter 5

A LONE VOICE IN THE WILDERNESS

God will take men through training to enhance their capacity before He entrusts them with greatness. On our way to the throne and obtaining a crown, we must be subjected to training that will help us develop the stature to handle the issues of the throne.

Student and the teacher

Our Eternal father is a very good trainer. Any person who ascends to power, authority, greatness, or throne without proper training will lack the ability to sustain them. People who ascended to greatness before passing through the wilderness training ended up in mediocrity because they could not handle power. The reason why some people in great positions are not making an impact is because they avoided the place of training which ended up making them half-baked.

Profit from the Pain

Someone once said that man does work for profit in order to enjoy pain; but in a positive sense, he works to enjoy the excitement and meaning that achievement provides for his own psychological growth and thereby his happiness. Every time we ask God for elevation and greatness, we are telling Him to expose us to the wilderness experience where capacity is built. As the proverb goes, "no pain, no gain." Some saints pray asking God to bless and elevate them but they do not know that the price of greatness is paid in the wilderness. When athletes are going to competition and they expect to be crowned as winners, they are exposed to intense training in very adverse climatic conditions to build the capacity to compete. No athlete will wake up in the morning and get into the race expecting a crown without having toiled in the process. They must endure the intense training for months to build the capacity to compete if they want to emerge winners. Athletes who are champions will lose their medals the moment they forsake training and rely on their former glory. The quality of the training determines the quality of results. The wilderness experience is a capacity enhancer.

God does not work with untrained soldiers

The Pain Points

In the armed forces, the soldiers undergo different trainings and the more intense the training, the higher the rank. For instance, if there is an attack from a dangerous terrorist group, the commander will not send traffic officers to the battlefield because they have not enhanced capacity to deal with terrorists.

Divine training hardens us to withstand any challenges that we face in life. The reason why the church is bringing forth believers without the stature to overcome the hardships and challenges of the world is that they have not been exposed to the wilderness experience. Before we spend years seeking God for prosperity and elevation, let us first seek divine training. The reason we are losing believers to the world is because they were not discipled well. The wilderness is part of the lessons that they must go through on their way to greatness. Many believers have been exposed to the prosperity gospel and when storms hit their lives, they have no capacity to hold on to their faith.

The wilderness borders the Promised Land

11Days vs 40years

An 11-day journey was covered in 40 years. Though anointed, Moses did not invest in teaching his church about building capacity. Consequently, God avoided taking them through the route in the land of the Philistines which was shorter.

> *Then it came to pass, when Pharaoh had let the people go, that God did not lead them by way of the land of the Philistines, although that was near; for God said, "Lest perhaps the people change their minds when they see war, and return to Egypt." So God led the people around by way of the wilderness of the Red Sea. And the children of Israel went up in orderly ranks out of the land of Egypt.*
>
> *(Exodus 13:17-18)*

Despite there being a shorter route to Canaan, God was aware of the dangers of accessing the Promised Land before an encounter with the wilderness to enhance capacity. The wilderness borders the Promised Land. The land of Canaan was inhabited by giants who were the sons of Anak. Since the Israelites had not been trained for battle, they needed a wilderness experience to train them and build their capacity to face the Canaanites, Jebusites, Hittites, Amorites, and Perizzites. After this exposure to the wilderness, only Caleb and Joshua qualified to crossover to Canaan in their generation. The Israelites had never experienced any war with another nation hence exposure to the wilderness trained them to face the days of adversity.

If we will raise a generation that will walk in greatness, then we must reveal to them the importance of enrolling in the school of wilderness. Moses was destined to be a deliverer of the nation of Israel; however, it took him forty years in the wilderness to enhance his capacity to stand before Pharaoh. Pharaoh was known to be a hard man, therefore, Moses needed exposure in the wilderness that could take away fear and equip him with boldness to confront Pharaoh. This exposure hardened Moses so that when the opportunity came to face the fierce Pharaoh, he did so courageously. The wilderness experience precedes Pharaoh's experience. God will not expose you to Pharaoh before the training.

Where is God when it Hurts?

Have you ever felt alone and forsaken by God? The earth is a spiritual battleground. There is no resting on earth. To triumph and survive when life baptizes us with fire, God exposes us to His tough training. When the Israelites were complaining of famine, fiery serpents, and drought in the wilderness, Moses was settled in mind because he had tasted the wilderness before. Some ministers ask God to walk with them but they don't understand the price attached to greatness. We have a generation that wants to use shortcuts to the top and is unwilling to enroll in the school of God's training where capacity is enhanced. What will keep you in the race is the capacity you have built in the wilderness. The wilderness is not a place of merry and pleasure but if we successfully graduate from it, we can handle any pressure in life. The Israelites were willing to return to Egypt and be enslaved because they lacked the stature to withstand the wilderness exposure.

God is with you in the training. It may hurt but it's worth it.

The measure of your capacity is determined by the scars of the wilderness you bear

Satan the Schemer

> *"When an unclean spirit goes out of a man, he goes through dry places, seeking rest, and finds none. Then he says, 'I will return to my house from which I came.' And when he comes, he finds it empty, swept, and put in order. Then he goes and takes with him seven other spirits more wicked than himself, and they enter and dwell there, and the last state of that man is worse than the first. So, shall it also be with this wicked generation."*
>
> (Matthew 12:43-45)

Satan is a good schemer. He will not attack before he is fully equipped for the course. Demons build capacity before attacking. In the passage above, Jesus revealed a mystery of how unclean spirits go to the wilderness to enhance their capacity so that they attack saints. The evil spirits are aware that the wilderness is a place of capacity-building while a believer is not willing to be exposed to the wilderness to build their capacity to withstand the powers of darkness. When God has delivered you from demonic powers, it is demanded of you to start building capacity so that evil spirits cannot overcome you. The reason the house is empty and the condition of the man worsens is that he never invested in building capacity. The reason why we have a generation that is unable to overcome the powers of darkness is because they avoid the wilderness before their capacity is enhanced. The sons of Sceva had no revelation that the two men had an encounter with the wilderness when they quoted Jesus and Paul to the evil spirit. The evil spirit responded to them in terms of capacity, that Paul and Jesus had the capacity to cast it out but not them since they had not undergone the school of divine training for capacity enhancement.

> *The greater the affliction the greater the anointing*

The suffering is working for you

> *Then Jesus was led up by the Spirit into the wilderness to be tempted by the devil.*
>
> (Matthew 4:1)

> *Then Jesus returned in the power of the Spirit to Galilee, and news of Him went out through all the surrounding region. And He taught in their synagogues, being glorified by all.*
>
> (Luke 4:14-15)

The ministry that Jesus was accorded was great and He needed an enhanced capacity to accomplish it. When God sought to redeem mankind, there was no one with enough capacity to carry that task apart from Jesus Christ. This assignment was not easy; it required enough preparation to be accomplished. Therefore, to carry out this task Jesus had to spend forty days and forty nights in the wilderness to build His capacity. Despite Jesus being God, He was not an exception to the wilderness school of preparation. If Jesus, our perfect example was not an exception, how then does a believer want to use shortcuts and avoid this school?

When Jesus was being led into the wilderness, He was not yet endued with the power to perform signs and wonders, but on His return, He had built enough capacity to accommodate the power of doing exploits. The anointing for exploits does not come on a silver platter, it is acquired by men who are sold out to God to enhance their capacity.

The Price Tag of Greatness

Great afflictions give birth to great anointing. There is no greatness that comes without paying the price. This price is paid in the wilderness. Jesus was not afraid of facing the cross which was a painful experience because He had already enhanced the capacity to handle it in the wilderness. It was after the experience in the wilderness that God anointed Jesus with power for influence. The grace to function extraordinarily is birthed in the wilderness. Upon walking through the wilderness and experiencing pain and adversity, Jesus received a crown and a name above every other name. The way to glory is the wilderness.

The way to glory is the wilderness

When Darkness Descends

This was the same training the apostles went through in the hands of their persecutors but the more they were persecuted, the more the oil kept on increasing. Jesus taught us that the way to become great and influential was going through the wilderness to enhance capacity. In the days of adversity and hardship, it is the capacity you acquired in the wilderness that will help you withstand them. The teachers of the law were rough and merciless but Jesus was able to withstand their pressure because He had an encounter with the wilderness. Shadrach, Meshach, and Abednego after passing the test in the fiery furnace, had their capacities enhanced to handle positions of governors in Babylon.

Daniel underwent the wilderness of accusation and the den of lions which birthed the capacity to be a leader of a province. When still a child, Jesus was hidden from Herod who wanted to kill Him because He had not enhanced capacity. However, when He had passed through the wilderness, He enhanced the capacity to conquer death. The fear of engaging in things comes because of lack of capacity to perform them. The wilderness is a place to strip off that fear. The wilderness is a place of pruning and extracting what limits our capacity enhancement to equip us with enough capacity for the next level.

Chapter 6

THE MEASURING LINE

Capacity building is a personal responsibility. God will not build capacity on your behalf. If we must provoke the flow of oil, then saints must invest in capacity growth. Elisha's first assignment to the widow was gathering empty jars. I believe that ministers should invest in teaching members how to enhance their capacities rather than discussing problems.

The Process

Building is not a one-day event, it involves many elements. There are things that we must do in our day-to-day lives to enhance our capacities. The men we admire enhanced their capacities to perform great things and understood some secrets that made them who they are. If the church does not understand these secrets, she will raise a generation with limited capacity. The reason people remain at the same level despite receiving prophecies of becoming great is because there is inadequate information on how to grow in capacity. God desires to fully maximize our potential but the actualization of this reality is hidden in the growth of our capacity. For three years in His ministry, Jesus chose twelve men and began to grow their capacity so that they would take after Him. The greatest assignment of Jesus towards His disciples was to help them grow their capacities and make them men of stature to turn the world towards the throne.

Educate

If Jesus overlooked the lessons on building capacity among the disciples, then His mission would have become a failure. A good shepherd invests in growing the capacity of his flock so that even in his absence they will be able to stand. The reason the apostles had the boldness and courage to preach the gospel without fear is because their master had spent time building their capacity because He knew what would befall them. The success of future generations will be determined by how well we teach them how to build capacity. In a changing world, the only way to adapt to these changes is through building capacity. The reason why the Israelites were afraid of facing the inhabitants of Canaan and were willing to return to slavery is because their leader Moses, never took quality time investing in their growth. Every challenge they faced reminded them of Egypt. They often complained to Moses of bringing them to the wilderness to perish there. Getting the Israelites out of Egypt was much easier than getting Egypt out of their minds. Though God had promised them liberty, Moses their priest hardly invested in teaching them about building the capacity to face the wilderness' turmoil and quagmire.

If we will attract God to release what He has in store for us, He must see the capacity we have built to accommodate the blessings. Frustration in life does not come because God is mean in blessing us but because the capacity we have enhanced is limited.

> *God does not manufacture greatness hurriedly*

How do we measure the level of our capacity?

i. Faithfulness with the little

God does not manufacture greatness hurriedly. He is a God of process. When we pray to God for mega blessings, He hears us but He first tests our faithfulness. After He has seen faithfulness with the little He has placed in our hands, He is moved to add more blessings. If we are unable to remain faithful with the little that God has given us then we limit our capacity to receive more. Some people have remained stagnant in ministry, business, job, and career not because there is an evil altar fighting them but because they are unfaithful with the little God has blessed them with. The degree of your faithfulness determines your capacity to receive from God. When God saw the faithfulness of Abraham, being willing to sacrifice his only son, God was moved to bless him with more descendants like the sand of the sea. Abraham never wavered on the promises of God. He walked in faithfulness before God and this moved Him to ordain him a father of many nations. Through him, a nation was established because he was faithful to what God had placed in his hands. When God wants to trust a man with greatness, He must take him through the test of faithfulness and his performance will determine his capacity to receive. We are living in a time where people are using dubious means to rise to greatness but many cannot sustain it because they failed to be faithful with the little.

From breakeven to breakthrough

When I began ministry in a small room in Mathare North-Nairobi, the voice of the Lord said that the numerical and spiritual growth of my ministry would be determined by my degree of faithfulness with the little. After a year of stagnation, I entered into a covenant of faithfulness with God; serving Him faithfully with fear and trembling. God loves us equally but entrusts us in proportion to our faithfulness. Heaven will not entrust you with a mega breakthrough until you are faithful with the little. I rationally adhered to this voice and today I can attest that the Lord has been faithful. He responds to our needs because of faith but growth in the Kingdom of God is directly proportional to our faithfulness.

Bottom-up

Every giant was once a child;
Every father was once a boy;
Every mother was once a girl;
Every leader was once a follower;
Every aged man was once young.

> *For who has despised the day of small things?*
> *(Zechariah 4:10a)*

Some people want to climb the tree from the top rather than from the bottom. God has blessed people with humble beginnings but they have ended up despising them and missed greater things that God had kept for them. Job reveals in *(Job 8:7)* that beginnings may be small but the end is increasingly great. However, to end up in increase and abundance, we must first prove to God that we are faithful with the little. Some men fall from great levels because they never built the capacity to contain greater blessings in the days of their humble beginnings. Job remained faithful to God even in His low moments and this triggered God to bless him with a double portion. There are people who were lifted by God in marriage, ministry, and business but lost the blessings because they had not practiced faithfulness with the small things God gave them.

Before asking God for an increase in your salary and wealth, examine whether you have been faithful with what you have first. One of the keys to great wealth and abundance is being faithful in giving and tithing in the days of humble beginnings. Some people struggle to give yet they keep on asking God to bless them with more wealth. Well in this case God will hesitate because He has not seen increased capacity. Our rise in the Kingdom of God is determined by the capacity we enhance through faithfulness.

> *So, he who had received five talents came and brought five other talents, saying, 'Lord, you delivered to me five talents; look, I have gained*

five more talents besides them.' His lord said to him, 'Well done, good and faithful servant; you were faithful over a few things, I will make you ruler over many things. Enter into the joy of your lord.' He also who had received two talents came and said, 'Lord, you delivered to me two talents; look, I have gained two more talents besides them.' His lord said to him, 'Well done, good and faithful servant; you have been faithful over a few things, I will make you ruler over many things. Enter into the joy of your lord.' Then he who had received the one talent came and said, 'Lord, I knew you to be a hard man, reaping where you have not sown, and gathering where you have not scattered seed. And I was afraid and went and hid your talent in the ground. Look, there you have what is yours.' But his lord answered and said to him, 'You wicked and lazy servant, you knew that I reap where I have not sown, and gather where I have not scattered seed. So you ought to have deposited my money with the bankers, and at my coming, I would have received back my own with interest. Therefore take the talent from him, and give it to him who has ten talents.

(Matthew 25:20-28)

Jesus wanted to teach His disciples how to build the capacity to trigger more blessings in the Kingdom of God. The master of the three servants understood the capacity of each of his servants and he distributed the talents accordingly.

> *God will hear prayers because of faith but He entrusts us according to the degree of faithfulness*

The test of faithfulness

The master was testing their faithfulness in multiplying what he had given them to see whether they had the capacity for more. When God is distributing His blessings, He knows our capacities differ from one person to another. The first two servants understood the key to multiplication and abundance is in remaining faithful with the little. Some people were ordained by God to walk in greatness but they failed because they became unfaithful with the little they had. The other servant remained without any progress in life, not because his master hated him but because he could not handle abundance. God has increasingly anointed and granted me much grace because I have a covenant of faithfulness in whatever He has deposited in me. Some men were instruments of greatness in the past and God used them mightily but today they are not on the cutting edge; not because they sinned but because they failed to remain faithful and instead of increasing in anointing, they diminished. The easiest way to lose the little blessings that God has bestowed on us is by walking in unfaithfulness. There are believers who have received one gift from God while others have ten. This does not mean God hates them but we must prove our faithfulness with the little He has given us. God will hear prayers because of faith but He entrusts us according to the degree of faithfulness. Our reward from God is based on our faithfulness.

ii. Capacity to handle pressure

A supervisor who struggles to handle the pressure of three employees has no capacity to manage double the number. A pastor struggling to manage a small church cannot handle the pressure of a mega-church. Until the capacity grows, no matter how prayerful you might be, there will be no manifestation on earth.

Chorus of Cicada

Our stature to handle the pressure at our current level

will determine our capacity to deal with pressure at the next level. Every level that God places us in attracts challenges and opposition; therefore, if we cannot deal with challenges at the level we are in, then we must forget the next level. God will try us in our current state to determine whether we are ready to handle the next. Many people are praying to God for elevation to greater dimensions but they are unable to withstand the adversity at their current level.

Our God loves us incredibly. The love is enormous to the extent that He would not expose us to positions and pressure that we cannot handle. An employee who struggles to handle the pressure of supervising a small group has not attained the capacity to supervise a larger group. No matter how much this employee prays for elevation, his promotion could be delayed because he has not exposed himself to build enough capacity that qualifies him to deal with a bigger team.

> *Therefore, we also, since we are surrounded by so great a cloud of witnesses, let us lay aside every weight, and the sin which so easily ensnares us, and let us run with endurance the race that is set before us, looking unto Jesus, the author and finisher of our faith, who for the joy that was set before Him endured the cross, despising the*

shame, and has sat down at the right hand of the throne of God.

(Hebrews 12: 1-2)

There was a crown of glory set before Jesus but to receive it, He had to develop the capacity to handle the pressure and pain of the cross. After enduring the pressure of carrying the cross, He qualified for the next level – sitting at the right hand of the Father.

The Adversity Quotient

God will allow us to endure fiery situations to develop the adversity quotient and build our capacity to stand before kings. Sometimes Jesus would let His disciples go without Him and storms would arise. His agenda was to ensure that they built enough stamina to confront the world in His absence. These trainings ensured that they could face imprisonment, persecution, and hardships for the sake of the gospel. When the mother to the sons of Zebedee wanted Jesus to favor her sons and promote them, Jesus revealed that receiving such a promotion was for those who were ready to handle the pressure of the cup of suffering and baptism of death. Jesus revealed that if you cannot share in His suffering then you cannot handle greatness. Before you seek God for greatness develop an immunity to handle the pressures that you are facing at your current level.

iii.   Capacity to Forgive

No matter how much you train human beings, they will always make mistakes which will offend you. In the journey of life, we meet with offenders who inflict pain and bitterness in our hearts. However, a bitter heart is a limiting factor in enhancing the capacity to receive more from God. Many people have failed to carry out great assignments and blessings from God because they have bitter hearts and are not willing to let go. The more we are unable to forgive people, the more we reduce the capacity to contain bigger blessings. Some ministers seek God for great power and anointing to serve God but heaven has not responded because they have held grudges. Unforgiveness is a sign that one has a faint heart and hence the capacity for greatness is limited.

The Test of Forgiveness

The men of God are tested in many ways and more so whether they have the ability to forgive. This is for God to ascertain whether they can accommodate other people's weaknesses. When God is on the journey of elevating us, He will allow those close to us to offend us in a bid to test our ability to forgive: If we fail then we miss the opportunity. If you are struggling to let go of the people who wronged you twenty years ago and you are asking God to grant you greatness, then you will wait longer.

The greatest pain is that inflicted by those that are dearest to you. Joseph was not suffering because of his neighbors or enemies but rather because of people related to him by blood. Have you ever imagined the people who should support your vision turning against you and seeking to finish you after revealing your vision to them? Betrayal from people who do not know you is better than that which is orchestrated by your brothers and sisters. This was Joseph's situation after telling his brothers about his dreams, they became jealous of him and turned their backs on him. Joseph had every reason to be bitter and detach himself from them but the man understood forgiveness is an enhancer of capacity.

> *Any blessing that we receive before enhancing our capacity is poisonous*

Don't revenge

Joseph was in a good position to revenge what his

brothers had done to him but his heart was ready to forgive. I have met believers who cannot talk to each other because they were offended and cannot let go. Such people have limited their capacity to receive more. The people you have vowed to never forgive because they offended you are the ones who are limiting your advancement. I have realized that the people we have chosen not to forgive cause more pain in our hearts. The proof that shows that you are ready for the next level is domiciled in your ability to forgive.

> *And when they had come to the place called Calvary, there they crucified Him, and the criminals, one on the right hand and the other on the left. [34] Then Jesus said, "Father, forgive them, for they do not know what they do." And they divided His garments and cast lots.*
>
> (Luke 23:33-34)

Jesus received painful treatment on the cross from the soldiers, yet He was without sin. Jesus did not take offence because He knew something greater awaited Him if He forgave them. The ability to let go is what made Jesus receive the capacity to sit at the right hand of the Father. If Jesus had not mastered the heart of forgiveness, He could have failed to accomplish His mission.

Forgive and release

The people you have vowed not to forgive are limiting your capacity to access the next level that God has ordained for you. Jesus spent time teaching His disciples the mystery of forgiveness because He knew a time would come when they would be offended and if they took offence, they would limit the working of God. There are dimensions of authority and power that God will never place us in if we are unable to forgive. I saw a certain minister friend seeking God for great levels of anointing but for years he remained at the same level. After asking God the reason why He did not want to promote him, God revealed that the man had worn a garment of unforgiveness. The people you have vowed never to forgive because they wronged and badly hurt you will be a stumbling block to your rising. In life, I have encountered betrayal and offence by people I trusted but God has taught me never to hold that against them in my heart. Capacity for the next level is determined by our willingness to forgive.

Pass the Test

Pass the test of forgiveness. I have not seen any man who God has elevated to greatness without passing the test of forgiveness. The same people healed, delivered, and fed by Jesus were part of the crowd that shouted 'Crucify him' but He went ahead and still forgave them. Stephen was stoned to death but even during his last breath, he did not carry offence. He asked God to forgive those who were stoning him for they did not know what they were doing. On our way to greatness, we will meet betrayal and offence but we must forgive to keep moving.

Chapter 7

WEAVE THE FABRIC

The greatest investment that preachers can make is teaching their disciples how to enhance their capacity. When Jesus called His disciples, He never released them to the field to heal or cast out demons. Instead, He stayed with them for three years training them how to build capacity for the assignment that was ahead of them. If Jesus had not taught them how to build capacity, then He would have produced half-baked apostles without the capability of changing the world. Whatever we receive before we have enhanced capacity will break us instead of building us.

> *Then He said: "A certain man had two sons. And the younger of them said to his father, 'Father, give me the portion of goods that falls to me.' So, he divided to them his livelihood. And not many days after, the younger son gathered all together, journeyed to a far country, and there*

wasted his possessions with prodigal living. But when he had spent all, there arose a severe famine in that land, and he began to be in want. Then he went and joined himself to a citizen of that country, and he sent him into his fields to feed swine. And he would gladly have filled his stomach with the pods that the swine ate, and no one gave him anything.

(Luke 15:11-16)

Jesus gave this parable to teach His disciples the importance of building capacity. The inheritance of these two sons was well kept and the father was waiting for the time his sons would enhance their capacity to give it to them. God knows the opportune time to release our inheritance because if it comes before capacity is enhanced, it will break us.

Pride vs Capacity

The father of these two sons knew they could not manage their inheritance therefore he was cautious of giving it before the right time. God will train and enhance our capacity because His agenda is not to break but to make us. According to the Jewish culture, inheritance was shared after the death of the father but the younger son decided to demand it before capacity was enhanced. This prodigal son could have invested and increased mightily in wealth but because he lacked capacity, he ended up eating with pigs. A man destined for greatness ended up a beggar because of a lack of capacity to handle greatness. Some believers seek God for greater blessings but after God blesses them, instead of rising, they fall into mediocrity because they have no room to contain the blessings. If you give a child power before they have built the capacity, they end up misusing it.

> *Whatever we receive before we have enhanced capacity will break instead of building us*

In the Interim

Jesus took thirty years building capacity for the assignment that was ahead of Him. When his mother Mary wanted Him to perform a miracle, He told her that His time had not yet come. Despite knowing He had the power to perform, He was cautious of His capacity. People who receive a small portion of anointing then step out before enhancing enough capacity end up failing miserably. The prodigal son could not handle greatness because he was not exposed to a capacity-building class.

Capacity for Inheritance

Apostle Paul says in *Galatians 4:1-2, "Now I say that the heir, as long as he is a child, does not differ at all from a slave, though he is master of all, but is under guardians and stewards until the time appointed by the father."*

Paul addressed the Galatians on attaining capacity so that they would be able to become heirs in the kingdom. Paul teaches that inheritance in the Kingdom of God is not given to children who have no stature. Some people are qualified to receive influence, greatness, and wealth but they are still children without the capacity. The greatest tragedy that can happen to a child of God is living like a slave yet he qualifies to own everything simply because they have failed to enhance their capacity.

The elder son understood he had not built the capacity to handle the inheritance and remained close to the father. Many parents have ended up spoiling their children by giving them inheritance before they have been prepared for it. Those who picked up before time have ended up failing in life because they had not invested in building capacity.

a. Ability to stay close to the Father

God's blessings are meant to draw us closer to Him. Jesus gave a parable of a man who had two sons. The younger (prodigal son) demanded his inheritance from the father. In *Building Capacity Vol 1*, I said whatever comes easily without a price leaves easily. When the prodigal son received his inheritance, he detached from his father and disappeared to waste his life with prodigal living. A Christian life has three stages: the prodigal son stage, the brother and the father stage.

> *Whatever has been birthed by divine presence must be sustained in this presence*

The Boiling Ocean

In the prodigal stage, believers are immature. Blessings move them away from the father instead of keeping them closer to him. Whatever has been birthed by divine presence must be sustained in this presence. Whatever it took you to rise is what you must keep doing to sustain the greatness. The younger son disconnected from the father as he was not mature enough to handle the received inheritance. This is a dangerous stage where a believer's fellowship with

God is negatively affected by their growth. It is risky to deviate once the Lord has elevated you. It is risky to celebrate the blessings you acquired from the altar in bars. It is risky to become a womanizer like the prodigal son after elevation.

The Test of Loyalty

In the second stage of brotherhood, believers are more mature. The father shared inheritance between his two sons but the elder son decided to remain close to the father. In this stage, believers have passed the test of loyalty and the Father can entrust them with more. A father sees the capacity in a son if every elevation draws him a step closer to him.

All the Father has is Ours

When the prodigal son came back, his father organized a party which irritated his elder brother but the father insisted that all he had belonged to him (the firstborn). You are entrusted because of your ability to remain close to the father. I made a covenant with God that every blessing and elevation will take me a step closer to the throne and nearer and dearer to Him. Glory to God!

The Missed Boat

The prodigal son had the opportunity and ability to continue receiving blessings from his father but this opportunity slipped away when he decided to stay far from the father. Sometimes what God gives us is not all that He has in store for us. God decides to test us first to see whether we can remain connected to Him. When God sees that His blessings have not taken us away from Him, He sees a person with increased capacity to receive more. God will give you a plot with an idea to give you wealth to build a house but when you run away after the first blessing, you limit the capacity to receive the remaining. When God had blessed Abraham with a son, He commanded him to sacrifice his only son. When God saw Abraham's commitment to remain connected with Him, He made him a father of many nations. The elder son understood everything he needed was in the custody of the father and he chose to remain close to him. Some people were very close to God when they needed a job, marriage, breakthrough, elevation, and success but immediately they received their desires they left the place of intimacy with God. The wealth, anointing, greatness, influence, breakthrough, and promotion you have received from God could be a test of how faithful you will remain in

His courts.

Remember where you came from

God delivered the Israelites from slavery and provided them with food and water in the wilderness *(Exodus 32: 1-4)*. However, instead of these people becoming more intimate with Him they chose to make an idol for themselves. God was testing whether they would remain connected to Him after fighting for them. Whatever takes you away from God is meant to limit your capacity to receive more from Him. The more we draw closer to God the more we provoke Him to draw closer to us. The prodigal son thought He would survive outside the presence of the father; he never understood his success was determined by how intimate he remained with him.

Whatever takes you away from God is meant to limit your capacity to receive more from Him

Nearer and Dearer

If the blessing made you busy for fellowship with God, it has reduced your capacity to receive more. When you remain connected to God, He will give you the wisdom to handle the little He has deposited in your life. David understood this secret of staying in the courts of God and this made him the most successful king in Israel. His success was not based on his skills or connections but on his desire to remain connected to God. The higher you rise in life the more intimate you should become with God. When we walk away from God, we not only limit our capacity to receive more but also lose His covering which will expose us to our enemies.

The grave error!

When the boy walked out of his father's presence, he lost his protection and ended up losing everything. What a colossal mistake! Every time the Israelites moved away from God, their enemies prevailed against them. This was because outside His presence they lost the covering of God. Some people are so committed to serving God because they are anticipating blessings but once they receive them they only seek God again when adversity strikes.

The vine and vinedresser

> *"I am the true vine, and My Father is the vinedresser.* ² *Every branch in Me that does not*

bear fruit He takes away; and every branch that bears fruit He prunes, that it may bear more fruit. You are already clean because of the word which I have spoken to you. Abide in Me, and I in you. As the branch cannot bear fruit of itself unless it abides in the vine, neither can you, unless you abide in Me. I am the vine, you are the branches. He who abides in Me, and I in him, bears much fruit; for without Me, you can do nothing.

(John 15:1-5)

Jesus taught His disciples about the mystery of remaining connected to the vine. Jesus revealed that outside God there is no fruitfulness.

The Pain of Pruning

The pruning process is bitter but the fruits are sweet. Jesus revealed the importance of remaining close to the Father which was for Him to prune us for more yields. The prodigal son had a chance of becoming more productive only if he understood the secret of remaining close to the father. Some once very wealthy people ended up in poverty because they ran away from the Father after receiving blessings. The Father understands our capacity and what needs to be done to enhance it so that we can receive more from Him.

When the disciples had returned with a great report of how they healed the sick and cast out demons, Jesus revealed the most important thing was to ensure their names were in the Book of Life. If we remain connected to the source of our blessings, we will never run dry, our cups will always overflow. Moses' capacity to lead the Israelites in the wilderness was developed in the place of intimacy with God. The moment we lose touch with the throne of God we lose the capacity to stand before Pharaoh.

Stay close to the Father

The elder son knew that to sustain the blessing you must remain in the environment that birthed the blessing. The reason why some people cannot sustain what God has deposited in them is not because of evil altars or village witches fighting them but their inability to stay connected to the Father. Jesus was able to sustain the anointing that God placed in Him throughout His ministry because He knew the dangers of abandoning the secret place. There are men of God who used to walk in signs and wonders but the moment they lost touch with the place of intimacy, the glory of God departed from them. This was the secret that Mary had when Jesus visited them. While Martha was busy cooking, Mary sat at the place of intimacy.

The apostles remained on the cutting edge and never lost relevance because they had enhanced capacity by ensuring they had daily communion with the supplier of grace and power. Adam and Eve were unable to sustain the blessings of God in Eden because the devil managed to disconnect them from the Father. Our capacity to remain impactful, relevant, and productive will be determined by our connectivity to the Father.

> *The moment we lose touch with the throne of God we lose the capacity to stand before Pharaoh*

b. Practice humility

The day you develop pride is the day you stop rising. Lucifer lost his place in heaven because of pride. In the Kingdom of God, our rising is determined by our degree of humility.

Decrease to increase

We increase by decreasing, therefore, if we want to create room for more blessings we must walk in the path of humility. Throughout the scriptures, men who walked in pride were limited in walking in greater dimensions with God. Pride is being full of self, taking

God out of the equation and believing that your success is a result of hard work.

Down to earth

Moses is an epitome and S. I. unit of humility.

> ***Then Miriam and Aaron spoke against Moses because of the Ethiopian woman whom he had married; for he had married an Ethiopian woman. So they said, "Has the Lord indeed spoken only through Moses? Has He not spoken through us also?" And the Lord heard it. (Now the man Moses was very humble, more than all men who were on the face of the earth.)***
>
> *(Numbers 12:1-3)*

Aaron and Miriam were concerned about why God spoke to Moses and not them. They tried to find fault in his walk with God and thought he did not qualify being the only one hearing from God. However, they did not understand the secret of having the capacity to hear God was hidden in Moses' humility. Moses could interact with God as a man talks to a friend because he had a secret that others lacked, humility. The capacity to walk with God like Moses did was birthed by his humility. God will not entrust His secrets to proud men. Some believers spend days on the mountain so that God can speak to them but He seems silent because His secrets are not revealed to prayer warriors but humble men. Miriam and Aaron were not enemies of God, but they could not hear from Him like Moses because when He examined their hearts they could never be at par with Moses in terms of humility. Moses had the capacity to lead a whole nation in the wilderness because he walked in humility. God will never allow some people to become leaders to even small numbers because they will retain the glory for themselves. If you are seeking God for elevation in ministry, business, or career, God must test your meekness before He qualifies you. Some people have remained in poverty and stagnated in the same position not because God hates them but because He knows once they are elevated, they will become proud.

The day you develop pride is the day you stop rising

Don't touch His glory

When Nebuchadnezzar received elevation from God and became successful, he forgot it was by the help of God and took the glory for himself. The king was reduced to an animal for seven years. The glory that belongs to God is poisonous to men. God will give you a little blessing to test whether you can still be humble. When you pass the test of meekness, He sees your capacity to accommodate more.

Divine opposition

A proud man is always under divine resistance. *James 4:6* documents that God resists the proud but gives grace to the humble. The capacity to accommodate more grace from God for ministry, business, and marriage is determined by our humility. Pride provokes God to oppose men as quoted in several scriptures including *Matthew 23:12.* The greatest tragedy in a man's life is realizing that God is opposing him. Pride limits the scope of our reception from God. Some men were graced in life and walked in greatness but ended up in pitfalls because they became proud. The prodigal son's mistake was allowing pride to master his heart when he demanded his inheritance and felt he needed his father no more. This made a man destined for wealth to become destitute as misfortunes befell him. As a believer, don't just be prayerful when you need God to elevate you. Failure to pray is the beginning of downfall. Pray and remain humble. Every time proud men try to rise in the Kingdom of God, He resists them. When God has lifted you, you will need humility to sustain you at the top.

Below the Salt

Though He was God, Jesus humbled Himself.

> *Let this mind be in you which was also in Christ Jesus, who, being in the form of God, did not consider it robbery to be equal with God, but made Himself of no reputation, taking the form of a bondservant, and coming in the likeness of men. And being found in appearance as a man, He humbled Himself and became obedient to the point of death, even the death of the cross. Therefore God also has highly exalted Him and given Him the name which is above every name, that at the name of Jesus, every knee should bow, of those in heaven, and of those on earth, and of those under the earth, and that every tongue should confess that Jesus Christ is Lord, to the glory of God the Father.*
>
> *(Philippians 2:5-11)*

Paul taught the Philippian church how to attain greatness in the kingdom. He gave the perfect example of Jesus Christ who was God but humbled Himself even to death to save mankind. This expression of meekness is what earned Him a seat at the right hand of the Father and received the name above all other names.

In June 2016, I visited a general of faith, a father in the nation of Kenya Bishop Paul Mutua at the House of Prayer, Machakos. I imagined of the long procedure I would have to undergo before seeing him, including a protocol team but what I saw blew my mind. I encountered a simple man, very meek and down to earth. Here was a man who had walked with God for decades and was full of God's presence. He offered me a cup of tea as he advised me on how to succeed in ministry as well as sustain grace. He is a man of prayer, so he imparted the grace of prayer upon me. Despite being old and greater than me, he was a hundred times meeker.

As he laid his hands on me, prophesying and making declarations on how I would become a kingdom giant, my tears flooded the floor. I desperately cried to God to give me the heart of humility. Pride attracts divine resistance. No man can succeed on earth if heaven is opposing him. Take care!

The glory that belongs to God is poisonous to men

c. Gratitude

Gratitude is the key to multiplication in the Kingdom of God. Ungratefulness gives us a sense of entitlement. This makes us believe God must bless us because we are His children. Whenever we thank God for what we have, we provoke Him to release more because He sees enhanced capacity. The prodigal son lost the grace to sustain the inheritance because his heart was filled with ungratefulness. The son felt he was entitled to receive the inheritance though it was not the right time. The Israelites saw the miraculous deliverance from the land of bondage including the supply of food and water in the wilderness but with all these, they still complained to God because of ungratefulness. This ingratitude cost the whole generation except Caleb and Joshua who had the opportunity to inhabit the Promised Land. The Israelites were full of entitlement for they believed it was God's responsibility to protect and feed them. Whenever we receive blessings from God and fail to thank Him, we put ourselves at a risk of losing them.

Where are the Nine?

Jesus met ten lepers who needed healing and because of compassion, He healed them (**Luke 17: 12-19**). While one saw that it was important to return and thank Him, the rest felt they were entitled to the healing. The nine lepers received healing and went their way but one grateful leper went back to give thanks which gave him wholeness. Healing and wholeness are different. Wholeness means you have been healed and restored to be just as before. The skin of this tenth leper was restored and he became whole again. Only one of the ten returned to glorify Jesus. Where were the other nine?

> *Nothing depreciates in the hands of gratitude*

Gratitude makes whole

Ten lepers were healed, and one was made whole. This is the state of many believers in the church. After receiving breakthroughs and blessings from God, they forget it is not about their prayer but God's compassion. Ungratefulness has a tendency to remove God from our success and achievements which limits our capacity to receive more from Him.

Anti-gratitude Virus

Familiarity is an anti-gratitude virus i.e. taking God casually. From the ten, only one leper returned to thank God. The man who returned to thank Jesus was not even a native but he understood the secret of thanksgiving. The moment you understand that a man can receive nothing unless it is given from above then you will thank God for whatever you receive. The depth of our gratitude determines the height of our rising in the Kingdom of God. Our next level in life is tied to thanking God for our current level. When we thank God for what He has done we remind Him of what He has not done. Before you complain to God about where you are, remember what you despise today is someone's prayer item. When you are complaining because of failure to receive a salary increment remember someone is praying and asking God to bless them with a job. You have not enhanced the capacity to be whole if you have not thanked God for the healing. When God has remembered you, do not forget to return with a heart of gratitude.

Don't forget His benefits

> *A Psalm of David. Bless the Lord, O my soul; And all that is within me, bless His holy name! Bless the Lord, O my soul, and forget not all His benefits: Who forgives all your iniquities, who heals all your diseases, who redeems your life from destruction, who crowns you with lovingkindness and tender mercies, who satisfies your mouth with good things, so that your youth is renewed like the eagle's.*
>
> (Psalms 103:1-5)

> "And now, O priests, this commandment is for you. If you will not hear, and if you will not take it to heart, to give glory to My name," says the Lord of hosts, "I will send a curse upon you, and I will curse your blessings. Yes, I have cursed them already, because you do not take it to heart.
>
> (Malachi 2:1-2)

David teaches us that men tend to forget the benefits of God in their lives. David had seen God grant him success and victory over his enemies and to continue enjoying this he mastered the heart of thanksgiving. This was the secret of winning all the battles he faced because he enhanced his capacity through gratitude. Malachi also reveals that a blessing from God can be cursed if we walk in ungratefulness. Thanksgiving is a command from God. When Jesus thanked God for the two fish and five loaves of bread, there was multiplication and five thousand men went home full. Gratitude is the key that gives us access to receiving more from God.

> *The depth of our gratitude determines the height of our rising in the Kingdom of God*

Gratitude births greatness

You will struggle to enjoy greater breakthroughs if you don't learn to thank God for the little ones you already have. Jesus enhanced this capacity for more through gratitude. Stop complaining about the small salary. Thank God for the little and increase capacity for increment. Nothing depreciates in the hands of gratitude.

CONCLUSION

When the widow cried out to Elisha to rescue her, the prophet of God ordered her to gather empty jars – build capacity. She desperately needed divine intervention but capacity was not yet enhanced. Before you command blessings that will make your cup overflow, ask God to empower you to build capacity for what you desire from Him.

God is ready to release. God is ready to make wonders happen. The releasing end is unlimited but the receiving end has limited capacity. Increase your capacity for the overflow of blessings.

You could be asking God to bless you with abundance, thank Him for the little you have and provoke Him to bless you with more. Thanksgiving births abundance!

BOOKS BY THE AUTHOR

 Every thing in the Kingdom of God happens within the realm of faith. It is total reliance and dependancy on God. Faith therefore is the backbone of Christian Faith. May the revelation herein trigger your faith to grow.

 No one is too busy to pray. Daniel was a busy Babylonian Prime Minister but that notwithstanding he spared time to pray. Prayer should be habitual. God is inviting us to constantly talk to Him through prayer.

 The cross was a place of divine exchange, restoration and victory. The fall of man in the garden of Eden propelled God to execute a plan to restore man to his place of dominion. The path of man's redemption was initiated by the death of Jesus on the cross. At Calvary it was restored.

 God reveals the great destiny in store for each of us, but rarely reveals the path we must take. Great destinies are accompanied by tough processes which help us to gain stature to handle greatness. This book will help to discover what you need to know about the how and what of your destiny!

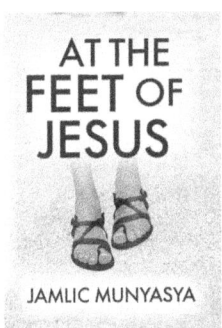 Relationship with Jesus is more important than anything else. The inward worship precedes the outward service. Our effectiveness in the secret place determines our impact in the public. One thing is needed, Mary has chosen that which will never be taken away from her.

 The blood of Jesus is the only divine blood. It carries the life of God. Its impact cannot be outdated-its power is from generations to generations. Obtain this powerful book to learn more about the Mystery & Benefits of Christ's Blood.

God will never release something that is beyond your capacity. We only attract what we can accommodate. Greatness here on Earth is directly proportional to the capacity one can accommodate. This book is the first of a series on this title.

In sequel to *Building Capacity Vol.1*, we delve deeper in this current volume to explore higher principles that we need to learn and apply in our lives to build capacity for growth and overflow. We must aspire to become the best versions of ourselves. Read this book and learn how to be the greatest you that can ever be!

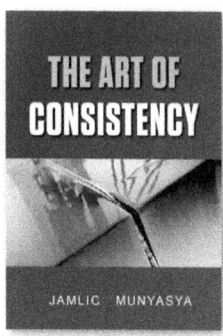

A one hit wonder! We have all heard about a singer who releases a great hit-only once. The problem is a lack of consistency and yet true greatness is in being great, always. That's an art we must learn and embrace. That is what this book teaches us to do: develop the art of consistency!

KOINONIA is about communion with our Heavenly Father. Genuine KOINONIA is that which originates from the heart. It's better to commune with a heart without words than words without the heart. The move of God is absent when we worship with our lips and emotions, yet our hearts are far off.

Excellence can be learnt and developed. It is a decision we make and live by. In this book, we walk through the journey of developing the spirit of excellence in our lives and walking in the same spirit. The book explores time-tested principles that we can all learn and apply in our lives to live lives that are defined by excellence. It will definitely change you!

Prayer is one of the most fundamental values of all the Christian disciplines! It is the most spiritual exercise that the human soul is capable of engaging in and yet simple. In this book, we look at this subject in a manner that will leave you with the desire to tap into the power that comes by and from prayer.

The kingdom of God is a kingdom of principles. One of the principles is that of gratitude. It is a potent force in the realm of the spirit. If you aspire to be great, don't fight mediocrity. Find the path walked by the great and walk it. This is an exposition of the various aspects of gratitude that will help you become intentional about living this lifestyle.

Faith is like wings of an eagle; it makes us soar to great heights. When fully embraced, nothing becomes impossible. In this book we explore the most central concerns in the subject of faith. The reader(s) shall not only know how to get hold of faith and grow in the same; but shall be challenged to apply faith in their own lives to move mountains.

We are products of our inner eye. Without dreaming, we live ordinary, and mediocre lives. However a dream needs a plan, strategy and clinical execution for it to come to fruition. Without cultivation and shepherding of our dreams, endless possibilities will all lie shattered. This book is important and urgent for everyone who dares to dream and pursue their destinies

All human relationships are fraught with conflict, misunderstandings, hurt and sometimes outright brokenness and damage because of wrongs that we all do to each other. If we do not forgive, families will hurt, marriages will fail, business deals will go sour, churches will break apart and whole societies will face turmoil! This book is a guide to help us open our eyes to the great need for forgiveness in all our dealings with each other. We have been forgiven; we ought to forgive! Find out why and how.

What do you know about the Holy Spirit? This book helps the reader to answer some essential theological questions in the simplest manner. The reader will get to understand that the Holy Spirit is a person in the Godhead, His work in the life of a believer, as well as how we can tap into His power.

There are times when life gives us a cold shoulder; roses develop thorns and things fall apart. Worst moments of God's silence were followed by overflowing seasons of testimonies. That's what this book is all about - testing for elevation.

www.ingramcontent.com/pod-product-compliance
Lightning Source LLC
Chambersburg PA
CBHW050307230526
45471CB00005B/2072